BLOOM'S ReViews

COMPREHENSIVE RESEARCH & STUDY GUIDES

Harper Lee's

To Kill a Mockingbird

Edited & with
an Introduction
by Harold Bloom

© 1999 by Chelsea House Publishers, a subsidiary of Haights Cross Communications.

Introduction © 1996 by Harold Bloom

Printed and bound in the United States of America.

The Chelsea House World Wide Web address is
http://www.chelseahouse.com

3 5 7 9 8 6 4 2

ISBN 0-7910-4168-9

Chelsea House Publishers
1974 Sproul Road, Suite 400
P.O. Box 914
Broomall, PA 19008-0914

Contents

Editor's Note

My Introduction asks whether *To Kill a Mockingbird* is a permanent work or a poignant period piece, and no answer is offered here. Critical Views begin with Harding Lemay, who argues that the idyll of childhood and the martyrdom of Tom Robinson are never meshed or unified in the novel. The book's dialogue and characters are praised by Frank Lyell and Richard Sullivan, respectively. Malcolm Bradbury, an eminent British critic, praises Harper Lee for her mastery of tone, while Nick Aaron Ford finds the portraits of the African-American characters to be persuasive.

An interview with the author by Joseph Deitch establishes her intentions as being regional and not merely local, after which W. U. McDonald, Jr., finds presages of Lee's novel in her college writings. Emerson is invoked by Fred Erisman, who finds Atticus Finch to be a singularly Emersonian hero.

The childhood aspects of the novel are examined and praised by William T. Going, while W. J. Stuckey rather refreshingly breaks ranks to indicate several of the palpable flaws in *To Kill a Mockingbird*. A somewhat severe judgment is made upon the novel's film version by Colin Nicholson, after which Claudia Durst Johnson concludes these extracts with a useful account of the elements that make the book another representative of American Southern Gothic.

Introduction

HAROLD BLOOM

The continued popularity of *To Kill a Mockingbird* (1960), a generation after its initial publication, raises, without answering, the crucial question about the novel. Is it only a period piece, charming but now outdated, or does it possess something of the stuff of permanence? It came out of our last Age of Innocence, the Fifties, before the Vietnam War and the upheaval of the Counterculture, and long before our current crises of race relations, economic dislocation, and failure of faith in government, indeed in all authority. Rereading it, after thirty-five years, returns one to an optimism about possibilities in human nature and in societal concern that many of us no longer share. Palpably, the book retains its pathos, but does it move us mostly through and by nostalgia? Is it now primarily a sentimental romance, touching but a shade childish, or is it, like J. D. Salinger's *The Catcher in the Rye,* another legitimate descendant of Mark Twain's *Adventures of Huckleberry Finn,* our classic romance of American childhood? Perhaps the questions can be summed up into one: Is Scout's narrative of her ninth year persuasively childlike, or is it essentially childish?

Jean Louise Finch, best known by her nickname, Scout, retains much of her charm as a classic American tomboy. She *is* indeed Harper Lee's book, being not only its narrator but much of its most interesting consciousness. Yet her deepest relation to Huck Finn, from whom she derives, is that like him she essentially cannot change. The crises of her book confirm her in her intrinsic strength and goodness, without wounding her sensibility or modifying her view of reality. Despite the villainous Ewell, and the conviction and death of the innocent Tom Robinson, a pure victim of Maycomb County racism, Scout retains not only her own idealism but her faith in the virtues of the people of her county. *To Kill a Mockingbird* comes out of an Alabama near related to William Faulkner's Mississippi, but in a cosmos apart from the world of *Light in August, As I Lay Dying, The Sound and the Fury,* and the other Faulknerian masterworks. Clearly it would be foolish to measure *To Kill a*

Mockingbird against the best American novels of our century, but is it wholly invalid to use Faulkner's vision of reality as a standard for reality testing in regard to Harper Lee's novel? Is her view of human nature adequate to a mature sense of the complexities of our existence? I myself am uncertain of the answers to these questions, but depending upon which answers prove right, *To Kill a Mockingbird* will someday seem either a sentimental romance of a particular moment or a canonical narrative.

A formal critic could argue in favor of Harper Lee's aesthetic restraint, since how could we strictly expect traumatic change in so brief a span of time for a healthy nine-year-old girl? Yet the voice narrating the novel is that of the grown-up Jean Louise, studying the nostalgias of her ninth year and chronicling events clearly more remarkable than she has known since. Whatever life has brought her (and she tells us absolutely nothing about that), she evidently is fixated upon what could be termed the era of Bob Ewell and of Boo Radley, would-be murderer and heroic savior, in her life and in the lives of Jem and of Atticus. That far-off era is a time warp, with a foreground but no afterground, from which we are excluded. And yet we can surmise that Boo Radley's heroic intervention was a decisive turning point for Scout, persuading her permanently of the benign resources inherent in even the most curtailed and wounded human nature.

To Kill a Mockingbird is an impossible book not to like; you can reject its idealisms, but the portrait of Scout Finch will linger on in you anyway. There are palpable formulaic elements in the book; even its largest surprises seem predictable enough. Still, the book is refreshingly free of ideologies and of the need to revise history to suit some particular politics of the spirit. The book's permanent importance, or lack thereof, turns upon Scout's personality and character. She is neither Huck Finn battling for inner freedom while dreading solitude nor (in a lesser register) Holden Caulfield defending himself against breakdown and madness. Motherless, she yet has the best of fathers in Atticus and the best of brothers in Jem. Most of all, she has her self, a will-to-good so wholesome and open that it charms nearly everyone she encounters, short of the brutal

Ewell and an officious relative or two. It is difficult to visualize a reader whom she will not charm, even at our time, in this place. Whether that charm will extend into days to come, I do not know. ✤

Biography of Harper Lee

Nelle Harper Lee was born on April 28, 1926, in Monroeville, Alabama, the daughter of Amasa Coleman, a lawyer, and Frances (Finch) Lee. One of her childhood friends was Truman Capote, who lived next door to her between 1928 and 1933 and would later become a celebrated novelist and essayist. In 1931 the Scottsboro incident occurred, in which nine black youths were arrested on the charge of raping two white women while riding on a freight train near the town of Scottsboro, Alabama. After several sets of trials from 1931 to 1936, in which some of the youths were sentenced by all-white juries to death, the case finally ended with several of the defendants being given long prison terms and others being released. Only much later was it discovered that the women had fabricated the whole story.

Harper Lee graduated from high school in Monroeville and then attended Huntingdon College, a private school for women in Montgomery, for a year (1944–45) prior to transferring to the University of Alabama. In 1947 she enrolled in the university's law school, later spending a year as an exchange student at Oxford University. She withdrew, however, in 1949, six months before she would have received a law degree and moved to New York City to pursue a writing career.

Lee had begun writing at the age of seven, and she had also written a variety of satires, reviews, and columns during her years in college. In New York, while working as an airline reservations clerk, she wrote several essays and short stories; none of these were published, but an agent encouraged her to expand one of the stories into a novel. Receiving financial support from friends, Lee gave up her job and worked on the novel *To Kill a Mockingbird,* which was a fictionalized account of the Scottsboro case and would be her only book. Although she spent much time shuttling between New York and Monroeville tending to her ailing father, she finished a draft of the novel in 1957. An editor at the publishing firm J. B.

Lippincott, Tay Hohoff, suggested revisions, and Lee rewrote the book. It was published in 1960.

The novel centers around Atticus Finch (whose last name is taken from Lee's mother's maiden name), a white lawyer who defends a black man, Tom Robinson, falsely accused of raping a white woman, Mayella Ewell. Although Finch's defense clearly proves his client to be innocent, Robinson is nonetheless found guilty by a white jury. The events of the novel are seen through the eyes of Finch's daughter, Jean Louise ("Scout"), and her brother Jem; Scout, as an adult, narrates the story as she reflects upon the events that occurred when she was between the ages of six and eight.

To Kill a Mockingbird was an instant popular success, even though early reviews were mixed: some critics found the work too moralistic, while others found the narrative of Scout's girlhood to be corrupted by her adult sensibilities. A year after its publication, the novel had sold 500,000 copies and had been translated into ten languages. By 1982, more than 15,000,000 copies had been sold, and the book remains popular among students and the general public. It won a number of awards, including the Pulitzer Prize, the Alabama Library Association Award, and the Brotherhood Award of the National Conference of Christians and Jews. In 1962 it was adapted into a noteworthy film in which Gregory Peck played the part of Atticus Finch. Lee was offered the chance to write the screenplay, but she declined; it was written by Horton Foote. The film won four Academy Awards, including best actor (Peck) and best screenplay (Foote). In 1970 Christopher Sergel's dramatic adaptation of *To Kill a Mockingbird* was published, and it has been performed widely throughout the United States and England.

Perhaps a further gauge of the popularity and importance of *To Kill a Mockingbird* is the number of attempts to ban or censor it. Many schools and libraries, mostly in the South and West, have sought to remove it from their shelves or from classroom curricula because it contains profanity, criticizes persons in authority, and displays other features that a variety of readers, both black and white, have found offensive on moral and political grounds. But all legal attempts to ban the novel have failed.

Harper Lee has been very reticent about her private life and about the sources for *To Kill a Mockingbird.* She has also written—or, at least, published—very little since the appearance of her novel, aside from a few autobiographical pieces published in 1961. She gave considerable assistance to her boyhood friend Truman Capote in the research for his "nonfiction novel" *In Cold Blood* (1964), jointly interviewing townspeople in Garden City, Kansas, who had known the Clutter family, which had been murdered in 1959. Capote dedicated *In Cold Blood* to Lee and Jack Dunphy. Lee began work on a second novel in 1961, but it has not been finished or published.

Harper Lee has received honorary doctorates from Mount Holyoke and the University of Alabama. She continues to live in Monroeville, Alabama. ❖

Thematic and Structural Analysis

To Kill a Mockingbird is set in Maycomb, Alabama, during the years 1933-1935. Maycomb is the kind of small Southern town where most families have lived for generations, nobody locks their doors at night, and the local telephone operator can recognize a person's voice without the caller having to identify himself. While the story deals with Atticus Finch's defense of an innocent black man, it is told from the point of view of his daughter Scout, and is as much about her life growing up in this tight-knit but racist community. The novel is divided into two parts: the first covers the events of the two summers and school years before the trial, and the second part covers the summer of the trial and takes the reader into the following autumn.

Because the story is told from a child's perspective (Scout, looking back "when enough years had gone by" still speaks in a simple and unaffected manner), the reader discovers the complex and inbred prejudices of Maycomb slowly, as they dawn upon the narrator. The full meaning of the novel's title does not emerge until the very end. The phrase is introduced part way through when Atticus gives Scout and Jem air rifles for Christmas. He tells them that if they intend to shoot at birds they must remember "it is a sin to kill a mockingbird." Mockingbirds cause harm to no one; they only sing for the pleasure of the world. Several of the novel's characters come to be associated with the mockingbird and as the story progresses Scout learns that it is these harmless and defenseless people whom the community is bound to protect.

The first of these vulnerable characters is the one about whom Scout and Jem have the most misconceptions. In **chapter one** Scout starts her story with the summer that she, Jem, and their friend Dill first try to make Boo Radley come out of his house. Dill is their neighbor's nephew who has come from Mississippi to spend the summer in Maycomb, and whom Scout and Jem immediately befriend. He is fascinated with the Finches' mysterious neighbor Boo Radley, who has never been seen to emerge from his family's house across the street.

Scout's style of narration is digressive and anecdotal, building up a rich portrait of the lives of Maycomb's residents. Her information about the Radley place is patched together from Jem's memories and from stories floated by the local town gossip. The Radley family had always been extremely religious—Miss Maudie calls them "foot-washing Baptists"—and when their teenage son got in trouble with the law they shut him up at home. Fifteen years later he stabbed his father in the leg with a pair of scissors and was taken to jail, but as Mr. Radley did not want him institutionalized, Boo returned home, never to be seen again. Stories proliferate about Boo who, once his father dies, is supervised by an equally repressive older brother. Petty theft and nocturnal pranks are blamed on him, children are frightened to walk by his house at night, and Jem describes Boo as a tall blood-stained ogre who drools and eats raw squirrels. All this is fuel for Dill's active imagination. The first summer he dares Jem to run up and touch the Radleys' house. Jem does so unharmed, much to Scout's amazement, but she thinks she sees a shutter move. This closes their first summer together.

In **chapter two** Dill leaves and Scout starts school. Through her perspective as a precocious first-grader (she has already learned to read sitting on Atticus's lap and sharing his newspaper) the reader begins to learn about the social strata of Maycomb county. Scout watches her well-intentioned but inexperienced teacher try to teach the rural children, all of whom come from dirt-poor farming families, rarely have the means to bring lunch, live complacently with lice and hookworms, and are held back year after year because of sporadic attendance. Scout, as one of the better-off town children, tries to negotiate between teacher and class, only to get in trouble herself. When she complains to Atticus he gives her a piece of advice which becomes a motif of the novel. He tells her to consider the other person's perspective, saying that "you can never really understand a person until . . . you climb into his skin and walk around in it."

As the disappointing school year draws to a close in **chapter four**, Scout finds two sticks of chewing gum poking out of a knothole in a tree at the edge of the Radleys' property. This is the first of a series of mysterious gifts that she and Jem find there. At first worried because of the proximity to the phantom-ridden house, they finally decide to keep the prizes. Meanwhile summer begins, Dill arrives, and the obsession with Boo Radley is rekindled.

Scout's first adventure takes place when the three children are playing with an old car tire and she accidentally rolls into the Radleys' front yard. She thinks she hears someone laughing as she flees in dizzy fright. Then Dill and Jem invent a game of play-acting the Radleys' story, complete with Jem impersonating Boo and his scissors-stabbing scene, until Atticus finds them and tells them to stop. Next (**chapter five**) Dill and Jem hatch a plan to give Boo a note inviting him out for ice cream, which they hope to deliver through the window on a fishing pole. Again Atticus discovers them and orders them to stop tormenting the poor man. Nonetheless, on the last night before Dill's departure they decide to risk all and sneak up to peek through the window. This time the older Radley brother spots something and fires a shot-gun in the air. In their rush to escape (**chapter six**), Jem's trousers get caught in the fence. Dill's quickness with lies saves them from Atticus and the sheriff, but Jem has to sneak back later to retrieve his pants. Instead of a vicious ogre waiting for him he finds someone has sewn his torn pant legs and laid them neatly back.

As school starts (**chapter seven**) more prizes appear in the tree: carved figures of Scout and Jem, chewing gum, an old school spelling medal and a broken watch. As Jem begins to suspect that the gifts must be from Boo himself, the older Radley brother, obviously detecting something, has the knot-hole filled with cement. Scout, who grasps less about the origin of the pres-ents, cannot understand Jem's despondency on wit-nessing this heartless repression. It is the first instance of an act of cruelty toward the weak and harmless, which will become a central theme of the novel.

Another theme that begins to develop is that of human courage and perseverance in the face of hardship and disaster. That winter (**chapter eight**) Maycomb county is hit with the first cold spell in years. Over the summer Scout has grown closer to her neighbor Miss Maudie Atkinson, who is a widow in her for-ties with "an acid tongue in her head" and a passion for gardening. She stands out as a sensible, understanding female role model in a world where ladies continually tell Scout to stop roughhousing and wear dresses. When Miss Maudie's house catches on fire during the first cold night in Maycomb the town comes out to help. They save her furniture but the house burns to the ground. Miss Maudie, staring at the symbol of all that she has lost, her twice-ruined "frozen charred azaleas," pulls herself up and declares that she had always wanted a smaller house: it will give her more yard space.

This episode is the last in Scout's childhood before the Tom Robinson case breaks, or before what she calls "a rather thin time for Jem and me." She first learns that her father is defending a black man when a classmate confronts her with the fact and she beats him up. Atticus prohibits her from any more fighting and tells her she has to learn to hold her head high and fight with her mind. He also explains that "every lawyer gets at least one case in his lifetime that affects him personally" and that this is his. He warns her that no matter how bitter people's feelings get, she must remember that they are still her friends.

The moratorium on fighting is difficult for hot-headed Scout. It is one of Atticus's first lessons for her on the importance of nonviolence, patience, and unprejudiced respect. Her self-control breaks down during Christmas vacation, which her family spends at the family plantation. In this episode in **chapter nine**, the reader meets Atticus's straight-laced sister Alexandra and playful, witty younger brother Jack. Also present is Alexandra's grandson, the (to Scout) much-despised tattletale, Francis. Scout learns from Francis about Alexandra's disapproval of Atticus. He tells her that "Grandma says it's bad enough he lets you run wild, but now he's turned out a nigger-lover we'll never be able to walk the streets of Maycomb agin." In a rage she attacks him; their fight is discovered, and Scout is forced to leave in disgrace. Her crime is partially redeemed when Uncle Jack learns the real reason for the fight and takes her side against Francis and Alexandra. Scout makes him promise not to tell Atticus, yet the reader suspects, as in so many of their childhood mishaps, that Atticus knows more than he lets on, choosing to stay out of their affairs when they can learn from their own mistakes.

The penultimate episode of Part I (**chapter ten**) presents Atticus in a stance that becomes symbolic for the rest of the novel. Scout and Jem have received air rifles for Christmas and their Uncle Jem has begun to teach them to shoot. Little do they know that Atticus was once the best shot in Maycomb county (he was nicknamed Ol' One-Shot as a boy). Then one cold morning Calpurnia, the family cook, spots a mad dog walking down the street. The whole town is alerted, people lock their doors, and Atticus and the sheriff are called in from work. As the rabid dog approaches, Scout and Jem witness a scene between the sheriff and their father. He asks Atticus to shoot the dog, telling him that it has to be felled in one shot without hurting the neighbors, and though Atticus protests, he takes the gun. To their amazement he walks calmly into the deserted street, drops his glasses, and shoots the dog directly in the head. This scene is invoked at later points in the novel: it symbolizes the town's dependence on Atticus's quiet courage and protection.

Chapter eleven is a coda to this lesson in bravery. The hidden protagonist is the Finches' neighbor Mrs. Dubose, a vitriolic, spiteful old lady confined to a wheelchair. Jem and Scout have to pass her house on their way to town, and every time they do she hurls insults at them. When she accuses Atticus of "lawing for niggers" and being no better than "the trash he works for," Jem loses control. On the way back from town he destroys her front lawn, cutting down every one of her camellia bushes. Scout is terrified: both she and Jem know he will be punished. When Atticus gets back from work he orders Jem to apologize. Scout thinks he is sending his son to certain death, but Jem returns to explain that he must read to Mrs. Dubose for a month after school in repayment.

Scout accompanies Jem on his daily mission, facing the hateful tongue of the sick old lady. At the end of each reading session she falls into a frightening drooling stupor. Yet the sessions grow longer and longer until Jem and Scout are finally relieved of their duties. A month later Mrs. Dubose dies. Atticus, who as her lawyer had put her will in order, explains to his children that with her illness she had been a morphine addict but that she was determined to die "beholden to nothing and nobody."

She had employed Jem and Scout to distract her while she fought withdrawal symptoms, holding off taking her medicine for a longer time each day. She had finally overcome the addiction altogether. Jem and Scout cannot understand how Atticus can call her a "great lady" and "the bravest person I ever knew" after she had continually slandered his name. Atticus explains: "I wanted you to see what real courage was, instead of getting the idea that courage is a man with a gun in his hand. It's when you know you're licked before you begin but you begin anyway and you see it through no matter what."

Atticus practices this kind of courage in the Tom Robinson case. He knows that it is impossible for a white jury to acquit a black man on the charge of raping a white woman, but he tries anyway. Yet because the story is seen through Scout's eyes this reality does not emerge until the verdict is reached. Part II (**chapter twelve**) begins with the arrival of summer and Jem's adolescent moodiness ("Mister Jem's growin' up," Calpurnia tells Scout). Scout also misses Dill, who has not come for the summer. When Atticus is away at the state legislature, Calpurnia decides to take the children to her black church on Sunday.

In this episode the reader is taken into Maycomb's black community, a separate neighborhood outside the town limits. They live in a much greater poverty than the white townsfolk: their church is bare and unpainted, and without organ or hymnbooks. Most of the congregation cannot read, so they sing hymns prompted by a reading member, who calls out the lines. Through Scout's young, unprejudiced eyes the service is seen for what it is: the gathering of a strong and tightly knit community. Aside from one belligerent woman who storms out, Scout finds the congregation warm and welcoming. At the end of the service the minister, Reverend Sykes, takes up a collection for Tom Robinson's wife Helen and does not dismiss church until ten dollars have been painfully collected. Afterwards some of the members stop Jem and Scout to praise their father. Scout leaves enthusiastic and amazed that her familiar Calpurnia has led such a different second existence.

Scout's enthusiasm is immediately checked in **chapter thirteen** with the arrival of someone less open-minded: Aunt

Alexandra, who has come to help take care of the children during this trying summer. Alexandra, who, as Scout observes, "had a way of declaring What Was Best For The Family," brings new tensions into the household with her opposition to Calpurnia, her insistence that Scout behave more like a girl, and her unspoken disapproval of Atticus's case. In the middle of one of the disagreements that ensues, Scout and Jem are sent to bed early. After fighting between themselves Scout retires miserably only to find what turns out to be Dill hiding under her bed. He has run away from his home in Mississippi. Happily, once his relatives have been telephoned and pacified, Dill is allowed to stay. Scout learns about Dill's lonely family life and realizes her own luck, despite all the tensions.

With the three summer friends again united the pace of the story picks up. The day before the trial Tom Robinson is moved to the county jail, and that evening Atticus quietly leaves for town, anticipating trouble. Jem is worried, so he, Scout, and Dill sneak out to follow. In **chapter fifteen** they find Atticus sitting by himself in front of the jailhouse. As they watch from a hiding place they see four cars pull up and a group of men get out. Atticus, unarmed, stands up to face them. As the men begin to threaten him Scout suddenly breaks away and runs to her father, Jem and Dill following. Atticus, shaken, orders the children to go home. Jem refuses. In the ensuing awkwardness Scout recognizes one of the men, all rural farmers, as the father of a classmate of hers. She tries, as Atticus has taught her, to engage him in polite conversation. Her genuine friendliness melts the animosity of the crowd—Atticus has, as she mentions, helped this very man with an entailment case—and they leave quietly.

It is Atticus's turn to be amazed by the effect of Scout's belief in human decency. "It took an eight-year-old child to bring 'em to their senses, didn't it?" he says the next morning (**chapter sixteen**). "That proves something—that a gang of wild animals *can* be stopped, simply because they are still human." This is the morning of the trial, and the whole county has turned out to watch. After lunch, Scout and Jem, against explicit order to stay home, collect Dill and head for town. Every seat in the courtroom is taken, and the children despair until they meet

Reverend Sykes, who takes them up to the black balcony. As the court is called to order the reader is introduced to the presiding judge. Judge Taylor, an old sleepy-eyed man who runs his court "with an alarming informality," propping his feet up and chewing on a cigar, is in reality learned and quick-witted. He is as eager as Atticus Finch to ensure a fair trial and see justice served.

The novel covers the testimony of the witnesses in great detail, spreading the day of the trial over the course of six chapters. Four witnesses testify: the sheriff, Bob Ewell, Mayella Ewell, and Tom Robinson. The sheriff, whom Bob Ewell called to arrest Tom the night of the crime, gives testimony that establishes two facts. First, no doctor was ever called to examine the victim, resulting in the state's lack of medical evidence of the crime. Second, Mayella was badly beaten on the right side of her face.

Bob Ewell's behavior on the witness stand (**chapter seventeen**) is contentious and disrespectful, and his language verges so often on the obscene that Judge Taylor is forced to reprimand him and repeatedly call the court to order. He testifies that he witnessed the rape through the window of his house but that Tom ran away before he could catch him. Atticus tricks him into proving that he is left-handed by asking him to write his name, showing that he could have been capable of inflicting the bruises on the right side of Mayella's face.

The next witness (**chapter eighteen**) is Bob's daughter, a timid spiteful girl of nineteen with little more than a second-grade education. Mayella is the oldest of a family of eight; her mother is dead and her father often drunk or absent. She claims that she asked Tom to chop up a commode for her the evening of the alleged crime, and that when she went into the house he followed her and raped her. Atticus manages through his cross-examination to draw out a picture of her lonely life as an outcast member of an ill-fed and uneducated family. It occurs to Scout that "Mayella Ewell must have been the loneliest person in the world. She was even lonelier than Boo Radley, who had not been out of the house in twenty-five years." It becomes clear from her frequent angry and tearful outbursts and her contradictory statements that Mayella is lying and trying to cover up evidence.

Her story contradicts Tom Robinson's, who next takes the stand (**chapter nineteen**). He is a tall, powerful man, but a crippled left arm hangs lifeless at his side. He tells of how Mayella, who claims not to have known him, had often asked him to do odd jobs for her on his way home from work. He felt sorry for her and was eager to help. He says that on the evening of the alleged rape she had asked him to fix a door handle inside the house. All her siblings were gone: she explained that she had saved for a year to send them to town for ice cream. The handle was not broken but when Tom started to leave she had stopped him, trying to hug and kiss him. He was resisting her when Bob Ewell saw them through the window. Tom had fled, justifiably terrified of the consequences. Because of his arm Tom could not have inflicted the blows on Mayella's face, and it becomes clear that with his kind, gentle nature he would never have taken advantage of her. Nonetheless, the solicitor ruthlessly cross-examines him to the point where Dill, watching, is reduced to tears and Scout has to take him outside.

They return to catch Atticus's closing statement (**chapter twenty**). He argues that there is no corroborative evidence to support the case, and that Mayella lied to hide her own guilt of having tried to seduce Tom. He lashes out against the state witnesses who "in the cynical confidence that their testimony would not be doubted" had stirred up racial hatred to win their case. He makes a plea for equality before the law and asks the jury in its own conscience to do its duty.

Jem is jubilant, convinced that the case is won (**chapter twenty-one**). He is surprised when the verdict is so long in coming. The jury does not reconvene until after eleven in the evening, but when it does it passes what seems the inevitable judgment for this Southern town—guilty.

After the blow of this disappointment the novel's characters take some time to sort out their feelings (**chapter twenty-two**). Jem is devastated, Scout bewildered. Atticus, exhausted, admits that he had expected the guilty verdict but he feels optimistic about their chances at an appeal. The next morning the family finds their kitchen filled with food sent from the grateful black community. Miss Maudie tries to comfort them by arguing that the jury's long deliberation was itself an achievement: "it's just a baby-step, but it's a step," she tells them. Atticus reiterates this sentiment in a later talk with Jem, but tells him the ugly "facts of life": "in our courts, when it's a white man's word against a black man's, the white man always wins." When Aunt Alexandra, in another talk with Scout, forbids her from inviting a poor white schoolmate whose father may have held the jury out for so long, she retreats to her room in tears, devastated by the social prejudices that rule her world. Jem tries to comfort her, but, equally upset, concludes, "I'm beginning to understand why Boo Radley's stayed shut up in the house all this time . . . it's because he *wants* to stay inside."

The next crisis comes in **chapter twenty-four** with the news of Tom's death. Word arrives in the middle of one of Aunt Alexandra's tea parties where Scout, profoundly uncomfortable in her starched Sunday dress, has been trying to make conversation with the ladies. Atticus comes in unexpectedly and calls his sister and Calpurnia to the kitchen. Maudie and Scout join them. There they learn that Tom has been shot dead trying to climb a prison fence. Calpurnia leaves with Atticus to tell Helen Robinson, and Alexandra momentarily breaks down, wondering when the case will end and the town let Atticus alone. Maudie comforts her by reasoning, "Whether Maycomb knows it or not, we're paying the highest tribute we can pay a man. We trust him to do right. It's that simple."

Tom's death is likened in a local editorial to the senseless slaughter of songbirds—one of the novel's clearest invocations of its title. Nonetheless, the incident dies down, and normal life resumes (**chapter twenty-five**). Unfortunately, one source of continued disturbance is Bob Ewell, who spits in Atticus's face the day after the trial and vows to get him, then makes attempts to burglarize Judge Taylor's house and harass Helen Robinson. Yet nothing violent happens until the night of the Maycomb Halloween school pageant.

Scout is enlisted to play a ham, one of Maycomb's agricultural products, in the school pageant (**chapter twenty-eight**). She disgraces herself by falling asleep backstage, missing her cue, and then wandering on at a particularly inauspicious later moment. Mortified, she keeps her costume on (an encasement of chicken wire covered with painted burlap cloth) and leaves with Jem after the crowds have dispersed. (Atticus and Alexandra have stayed at home.)

Crossing the darkened school yard next to the Radley lot, Jem and Scout hear footsteps following them. Just as they reach the end of the yard someone attacks Scout, whose fluorescent painted costume makes her a vulnerable target. In the confusing scuffle Scout hears Jem, who runs to her rescue, being thrown off and then feels herself being crushed. Suddenly her attacker is pulled off and she follows in confusion as someone carries Jem back to the Finches' house. Jem is unconscious and his arm has been broken while Scout, because of her protective costume, is unharmed. The sheriff is called and he finds Bob Ewell lying dead in the school yard, stabbed with a kitchen knife. Meanwhile, Scout realizes that the tall pale man who has saved Jem is none other than Boo Radley.

When Atticus learns of Ewell's murder in **chapter twenty-nine**, he assumes that Jem (now unconscious under a sedative) must have done it. The sheriff wants to close the case by claiming that Ewell fell on his own knife, but Atticus's conscience will not·allow this. Stubbornly they argue as Boo and Scout look on. Finally the sheriff forces Atticus to see that it was Boo who saved the children by stabbing Ewell, and that he cannot in good conscience make this public knowledge. "To my way of thinkin', Mr. Finch," he tells Atticus, "taking the one man who's done you and this town a great service an' draggin' him with his shy ways into the limelight—to me, that's a sin." Atticus agrees and quietly thanks Boo for saving his children. Then Scout, no longer afraid of her childhood phantom, takes him in to see Jem and escorts him home (**chapter thirty**). Standing on the Radleys' doorstep she suddenly experiences what her father had tried to teach her: to stand in somebody else's shoes and walk around in them. She sees the street as Boo must have seen it, watching Scout and Jem playing and growing up, and understands how he acquired his affection for them and came to their rescue when he heard them in danger. The novel ends on this note of resolution in **chapter thirty-one**: Scout never sees Boo Radley again, but she knows that at least this mockingbird figure, who came to her rescue in a time of need, has been saved from public scandal and allowed to live his life in peace.

Thus, although the summer's trial has taught Scout that racial prejudice will cloud the moral judgment of many of her towns-folk, the message of Harper Lee's novel is by no means purely negative. Scout also learns that some Maycomb residents believe in human decency and the protection of the weak and defenseless—people like the sheriff, Judge Taylor, and Miss Maudie. Boo Radley, by defending Jem and Scout, acted out of this same impulse, despite his own stigmatization as a spook and an outcast. She also learns that with enough courage and conviction you can fight against racial prejudice, as her father has done, one step at a time. ❖

—*Anna Guillemin*
Princeton University

List of Characters

Jean Louise (Scout) Finch is the narrator of *To Kill a Mockingbird*. She relates the events of her life between the ages of six and nine when her father, a small-town Southern lawyer, is called to defend an innocent black man. The setting is Maycomb, Alabama, in the early 1930s. Scout is a combative tomboy and sharp, sensitive observer who lives with her widowed father, her older brother, and the family's black cook. In this coming-of-age story her father's trial teaches her about the indigenous racism of her community but also about the strength of her father's quiet courage, which she learns to value above her own angry impulsiveness.

Jeremy (Jem) Finch is Scout's brother, four years her senior and a comrade in most of her adventures. Scout watches him grow up during the course of the story, entering adolescence and abandoning the children's games they had shared together. Although he is occasionally critical, he remains a protective and close companion. The racism and miscarriage of justice he witnesses during the trial shakes his faith in the criminal justice system. Nonetheless, because of the role model of his father he hopes to grow up to be a lawyer and a gentleman.

Atticus Finch is Scout and Jem's father. Coming from an old Maycomb family, he has worked in town as a lawyer all his adult life. Widowed and nearly fifty, he is older than most of the Maycomb parents, but deeply admired by his two children. When he takes on the case of a black man wrongly accused of raping a white woman he is denounced by most of the townspeople as a black sympathizer but does not waver in his resolve. As Miss Maudie, a family friend, tells Scout and Jem: "There are some men in this world who were born to do our unpleasant jobs for us. Your father's one of them."

Calpurnia (Cal) is the family's black cook, who has brought up Jem and Scout. She is a strict disciplinarian with whom Scout has many run-ins, yet underneath her sharpness she loves the children dearly. Cal bridges the two worlds of the novel, fitting into both the educated white family (unlike most of the black community she can read and write) and the poor black shanty town where she lives. During the course of the story Scout realizes how important Cal is to her family and how different her life is outside the Finch home.

Charles Baker (Dill) Harris is Scout and Jem's best friend, who enters the story the summer of Scout's sixth year when he comes to spend three months with his aunt in Maycomb. Seven years old at the time, he is small for his age and looks like a misfit with his odd snow-white hair. Dill continually plays the clown, hatching stories, telling lies, and laughing easily. Underneath he is a lonely fatherless child, unwanted by his mother and stepfather and continually shuttled from relative to relative. He shares in Scout and Jem's adventures during the three summers he spends in Maycomb.

Arthur (Boo) Radley is the Finches' mysterious neighbor. According to town legend, he has lived locked up in the family house since the time when, as a teenager, he had a run-in with the law. When he was thirty-three, the story goes, he stabbed his father in the leg with a pair of scissors. He was temporarily locked up in the jail, but then brought home again, never to be seen outside. By the time Scout is old enough to remember, Boo's father has died and an older brother has come to watch over him. The local children are terrified of the Radley Place and imagine Boo to be a bloodthirsty ogre. Scout, Jem, and Dill are frightened but fascinated and repeatedly try to catch a glimpse of him or lure him outside. Little do they realize that Boo has come to regard them affectionately from watching them grow up. At the end of the story Boo comes to Scout's rescue, and she understands that the bogeyman she has always imagined is really a shy, gentle human being.

Tom Robinson is the black man wrongfully accused of raping a white woman. He is a strong, handsome man in his twenties with a wife and three children whose left arm has been crippled in a childhood accident. This disability makes it impossible for him to have committed the crime, a fact that the all-white jury ignores in handing him the death sentence. Despairing of any chance for an appeal (which Atticus thinks he has), Tom tries to escape prison and is shot to death.

Robert E. Lee (Bob) Ewell, the father of Mayella, the alleged rape victim, is the man who charges Tom Robinson with the crime. Coming from the poorest class of white subsistence farmers, he is an unemployed drunk, dependent on town charity, whose family lives in squalor next to the town dump. His eight children are sickly, underfed, uneducated, and often beaten. Evidence from the trial shows that Bob probably beat his daughter unconscious when he found her making romantic overtures to Tom, and then blamed Tom for the crime, knowing a white jury could not fail to convict him. He is an angry, brutish man who seeks revenge on Atticus for standing up against him in the courtroom.

Aunt Alexandra is Atticus's older sister who comes to live with the family the summer of the trial. She "fit[s] into the world of Maycomb like a hand into a glove," epitomizing the small-town Southern lady with her tea parties and missionary circles. She is also determined to make Scout into a little lady. Scout resents her intrusion, but during the trying events of the summer they are brought closer together and learn to respect each other.

Miss Maudie is the Finches' neighbor, a widow in her forties and an old family friend who serves as another role model for Scout. She treats Scout and Jem like adults instead of talking down to them, and she shows perseverance in the face of trial when her entire house burns down during a particularly harsh winter. Along with Atticus she is one of the characters who has the best perspective on the indigenous racism of the town. ❖

Critical Views

[Harding Lemay (b. 1922) is a playwright and television writer who has written *Inside, Looking Out: A Personal Memoir* (1971) and *Eight Years in Another World* (1981), an account of his writing for soap operas. In this review, Lemay believes that the two themes of *To Kill a Mockingbird*—Scout Finch's recollections of her childhood and Atticus Finch's defense of Tom Robinson—do not mesh, thereby failing to produce a unified impression upon the reader.]

In her first novel, *To Kill a Mockingbird*, Harper Lee makes a valiant attempt to combine two dominant themes of contemporary Southern fiction—the recollection of childhood among village eccentrics and the spirit-corroding shame of the civilized white Southerner in the treatment of the Negro. If her attempt fails to produce a novel of stature, or even of original insight, it does provide an exercise in easy, graceful writing and some genuinely moving and mildly humorous excursions into the transient world of childhood.

Set during the depression, the story is recalled from the distance of maturity by Jean Louise ("Scout") Finch, whose widowed father, Atticus, was a civilized, tolerant lawyer in a backward Alabama town. An older brother, Jem, and a summer visitor from Mississippi, Dill, share Scout's adventures and speculations among figures not totally unfamiliar to readers of Carson McCullers, Eudora Welty, and Truman Capote. The three children, supervised by an intelligent, perceptive Negro housekeeper, Calpurnia, play their games of test and dare with ill-tempered old ladies, buzzing village gossips, and, most especially, with the mysterious occupant of the house next door who has never been seen outside since his father locked him up over fifteen years earlier. It is through Boo Radley, whose invisible presence tantalizes the children, that Miss Lee builds the most effective part of her novel: an exploration of the caution and curiosity between which active children expend their energies and imaginations.

In the second half of the novel, Atticus defends a Negro accused of raping a white girl. The children add to their more innocent games that of watching a Southern court in action. They bring to the complexities of legal argument the same luminous faith in justice that sweeps through their games, and they watch, with dismay and pain, as the adult world betrays them. And here, perhaps because we have not been sufficiently prepared for the darkness and the shadows, the book loses strength and seems contrived. For everything happens as we might expect. The children are stained with terror and the knowledge of unreasoning hatreds but gain in insight and in compassion, and the author, deliberately using Atticus and an elderly widow as mouthpieces, makes her points about the place of civilized man in the modern South.

The two themes Miss Lee interweaves throughout the novel emerge as enemies of each other. The charm and wistful humor of the childhood recollections do not foreshadow the deeper, harsher note which pervades the later pages of the book. The Negro, the poor white girl who victimizes him, and the wretched community spirit that defeats him, never rise in definition to match the eccentric, vagrant, and appealing characters with which the story opens. The two worlds remain solitary in spite of Miss Lee's grace of writing and honorable decency of intent.

—Harding Lemay, "Children Play; Adults Betray," New York Herald Tribune Book Review, 10 July 1960, p. 5

FRANK H. LYELL ON HARPER LEE'S DIALOGUE

[Frank H. Lyell is a former professor of English at the University of Texas and the author of *A Study of the Novels of John Galt* (1942). In this review, Lyell praises the dialogue of *To Kill a Mockingbird* as being both authentic and piquant.]

The dialogue of Miss Lee's refreshingly varied characters is a constant delight in its authenticity and swift revelation of personality. The events connecting the Finches with the Ewell-Robinson lawsuit develop quietly and logically, unifying the plot and dramatizing the author's level-headed plea for interracial understanding. At the trial, good-for-nothing Bob Ewell testifies that he returned one day to his shack by the local garbage dump to find his daughter Mayella "screamin' fit to beat Jesus" because Tom Robinson was attacking her. Mayella, however, was the assailant, after luring Tom inside to take down a box from a high chifforobe. She screamed because her father beat her unmercifully after Tom ran away. Nevertheless, Tom is convicted and later shot in attempting to escape from a prison farm. "Typical of a nigger to cut and run," most people think, but Maycomb's sympathetic newspaper editor agrees with Atticus in comparing Tom's death to "the senseless slaughter of songbirds by hunters and children."

The praise Miss Lee deserves must be qualified somewhat by noting that oftentimes Scout's expository style has a processed, homogenized, impersonal flatness quite out of keeping with the narrator's gay, impulsive approach to life in youth. Also, some of the scenes suggest that Miss Lee is cocking at least one eye toward Hollywood. Moviegoing readers will be able to cast most of the roles very quickly, but it is no disparagement of Miss Lee's winning book to say that it could be the basis of an excellent film.

—Frank H. Lyell, "One-Taxi Town," *New York Times Book Review*, 10 July 1960, p. 18

RICHARD SULLIVAN ON THE VIVID CHARACTERS OF *TO KILL A MOCKINGBIRD*

[Richard Sullivan (1908–1981) was for many years a professor of English at the University of Notre Dame and wrote a history of the college, *Notre Dame* (1951) along with several novels. In this review, Sullivan finds all the characters in *To Kill a Mockingbird* skillfully portrayed and the novel as a whole vividly told.]

⟨. . .⟩ this is a novel absolutely loaded with people: the gentle young Negro falsely accused and, even tho Atticus defends him nobly in court, unjustly convicted of rape; the sheriff; the judge; the jurors; some school children; a Negro minister; certain members of a ladies' missionary society, anxious about far-off affairs but blind to local horrors.

The style is bright and straightforward; the unaffected young narrator uses adult language to render the matter she deals with, but the point of view is cunningly restricted to that of a perceptive, independent child, who doesn't always understand fully what's happening, but who conveys completely, by implication, the weight and burden of the story.

There is wit, grace, and skill in the telling. From the narrator on, every person in the book is every moment alive in time and place. Maycomb, Ala., itself comes alive, as a town abundantly inhabited by individual human beings, each one possessed of his or her own thoroly convincing nature and personality. And each one contributes to the quiet, sustained humor, the occasionally intense drama, the often taut suspense which all rise out of this rich and variegated complex of human relationships.

Gradually, the novel unfolds and reveals not only a sharp look at a number of people but a view of the American south, and its attitudes, feelings, and traditions. Two grave problems of moral import are posed. One, involving an innocent Negro, is disastrously worked out, after due process of law. The other, involving the murder of a villain by a lunatic, both white, is worked out with amiable justice.

—Richard Sullivan, "Engrossing First Novel of Rare Excellence," *Chicago Sunday Tribune Magazine of Books,* 17 July 1960, p. 1

❖

MALCOLM BRADBURY ON HARPER LEE'S MORAL FOCUS

[Malcolm Bradbury (b. 1932) is a widely published novelist and critic and the author of *The Social Context of Modern English Literature* (1971), *The Modern American Novel* (1983; rev. 1993), monographs of Evelyn Waugh (1964) and Saul Bellow (1982), and many other works. In this review, Bradbury finds Harper Lee's moral focus clear-cut in its distinguishing of good and evil.]

Harper Lee in her first novel has turned to a recurrent theme, the theme of the guilt felt by the white man for what he has done to the negro. She also chooses to tell her story through the eyes of children, a strategy that I cannot normally bear because it prevents an adequate moral judgment on the fable. But Miss Lee has taken her risks and emerged triumphant. What is so good about *To Kill a Mockingbird* is not the substance but the tone with which it is treated. The story becomes a truthful tale about the difficulties of living well in a world where ignorance and prejudice make inroads on human decency. She understands her social scene, the American South; but her gallery of people has moral as well as social relevance. The good stands out from the bad at all levels. There is a splendid comic scene where the narrator, a young girl, goes to school for the first time and is taught by a Dewey-trained schoolteacher who spanks her because she is too intelligent and not one of The Group. But the point is made; intelligence and decency are positive values and this is why Miss Lee is such a good novelist.

—Malcolm Bradbury, [Review of *To Kill a Mockingbird*], *Punch*, 26 October 1960, p. 612

NICK AARON FORD ON HARPER LEE'S PORTRAYAL OF BLACK AMERICANS

[Nick Aaron Ford (1904–1982) was a leading black American critic who wrote *The Contemporary Negro*

Novel: A Study in Race Relations (1936), *Black Studies: Threat-or-Challenge* (1973), and other works. In this extract, Ford believes that Harper Lee has portrayed black Americans in her novel in an honest, nonstereotypical way.]

To Kill a Mockingbird by Harper Lee, born and bred in Alabama, is the complete antithesis of *Seed in the Wind*. Instead of stereotyped Negroes, this novel presents living, convincing characters—neither saints nor devils, neither completely ignorant or craven or foolish, nor completely wise or wholly courageous. Instead of blatant propaganda from beginning to end, the socially significant overtones do not begin to appear until the story has progressed a third of the way and then they creep in unobtrusively, as natural as breathing.

The story is really about a white Alabama lawyer named Atticus Finch and his efforts to raise his young son and daughter in such a way that they will always seek to know right from wrong and when they have discovered the right, or the truth, to live by it regardless of the cost. In his efforts to practice the creed he has adopted for himself and his children, he is faced with the task of defending a Negro falsely accused of raping a white girl. The most exciting part of the book deals with the temporary hate aroused against himself and his children in the typically Southern community as he steadfastly seeks and presents the truth of the case to the dismay of those who do not wish to accord the Negro equality before the law. Although his client is convicted, notwithstanding conclusive evidence to the contrary, and later killed attempting to escape the jailers, his action in the face of intimidation, abuse, and violence against himself and his children finally arouses such a sense of decency in the community that it would be unlikely that another such travesty of justice could ever happen there.

The story is told by Jean Louise Finch, Atticus' daughter, aged six at the beginning and eight at the end. It is dominated by the daughter's complete love and devotion for her father and older brother, her admiration for a boy her own age, her acceptance of Negroes as fellow human beings with the same rights and privileges as those of white people, and her hatred of all hypocrisy and cant. Her dramatic recital of the joys, fears, dreams, misdemeanors, and problems of her little circle of friends and enemies gives the most vivid, realistic, and delightful experiences of a child's world ever presented by an American novelist, with the possible exception of Mark Twain's *Tom Sawyer* and *Huckleberry Finn.*

The author's contribution to a healthy social sensitivity among her readers is twofold. Indirectly it reveals itself in the quiet dignity and wisdom of the Finch's cook and housekeeper, Calpurnia, in her dealings with the children of the household and the white and Negro adults of the community; in the anti-social, uncultured conduct of white school children, as well as adults, of low socio-economic status; in the conversion of aloof, undemonstrative citizens to active participation in the struggle for elementary human rights when abuses become flagrant and unbounded. It is revealed directly in such passages as the following, which quotes Atticus' comment to his thirteen-year-old son who is greatly disturbed because a jury has convicted an innocent Negro:

> The one place where a man ought to get a square deal is in a courtroom, be he any color of the rainbow, but people have a way of carrying their resentments right into a jury box. As you grow older, you'll see white men cheat black men every day of your life, but let me tell you something and don't you forget it—whenever a white man does that to a black man, no matter who he is, how rich he is, or how fine a family he comes from, that white man is trash.

> —Nick Aaron Ford, "Battle of the Books: A Critical Survey of Significant Books by and about Negroes Published in 1960," *Phylon* 22, No. 2 (Summer 1961): 122-23

JOSEPH DEITCH ON THE AUTOBIOGRAPHICAL ELEMENTS IN *TO KILL A MOCKINGBIRD*

[Harper Lee attracted tremendous publicity when her novel became a best-seller and won the Pulitzer Prize.

To the journalist Joseph Deitch, who interviewed her in New York City, Lee confesses that *To Kill a Mockingbird* is not explicitly autobiographical but does draw upon her upbringing in Monroeville, Alabama.]

Miss Lee is a tall, robust woman with a winsome manner, a neighborly handshake, and a liking for good, sensitive talk about people and books and places like Monroeville, Ala., her home town.

Monroeville is tiny, and was tinier when Miss Lee first got to know it, in the middle 1930's, she said, stirring her cup. It was pretty much the "one-taxi town" in her novel, and hearing about it contrasted oddly with the traffic noise coming up from Fifth Avenue.

You not only know everybody in Monroeville but are virtually "kin to everyone." It was a sleepy place before Miss Lee left it to go to college, but is lively now, thanks, apparently, to a national underwear mill that opened there.

It has also produced a gifted new American writer, who stressed that *To Kill a Mockingbird,* about a highly respected Southern lawyer and legislator who defies racial tradition, is not autobiographical, although it may read that way. Miss Lee tried hard to put on record a universal and classical "slice of life." She believes the book's setting could have been the Mississippi Delta, Georgia, or west Florida—"people are people anywhere you put them." It is her hope that all Southern readers of her novel will say: This is my town.

That she is achieving this aim is shown partly by the response of Monroeville itself to the novel and its success. "People at home have been extremely nice—embarrassingly so," she reported. What makes this local approval more interesting is that Harper Lee believes a writer "should write about what he knows and write truthfully."

Creatively, her goal was to develop a story as close to the truth as possible about an era and its people. She remembers the middle '30's as hard years in her region, but it was also a time when men and women and children lived simply and truthfully—truth is a word that comes up often as Miss Lee talks about herself as a writer and about things that matter most to her.

There were no "strivers" in those days—"life was grim for many people, who were not only poor but hungry, and their wants were absolutely basic," she said.

And so, with grace and power and courage, Miss Lee has re-created and champions a man like Atticus Finch for these days. Atticus, as he is referred to in the story, is the lawyer and central figure in her story. Miss Lee said he is a man of "absolute integrity, with as much good will and good humor" as he is just and humane. ⟨. . .⟩

Miss Lee is working on a second novel. Her day starts at noon—she sleeps late—and she writes until early evening. It takes her that long to write about a page. Before quitting, she types a final clean copy, "picking out the nut from the shell" as she types.

Like most writers, Miss Lee can talk about her work habits, broad objectives, and beliefs as a writer, and perhaps a little about why she writes as she does. She is almost stopped cold when asked to tell how you actually shape words into a book. Proof of this was her reaction to a letter she received from a 13-year-old girl.

"I have read and admired *To Kill a Mockingbird* and have decided," the girl announced, "to become a writer—what do I do?"

Miss Lee shook her head and chuckled unhappily.
> —Joseph Deitch, "Harper Lee: Novelist of South," *Christian Science Monitor,* 3 October 1961, p. 6

W. U. McDONALD, JR. ON HARPER LEE'S COLLEGE WRITINGS

[Little attention has been paid to the stories, articles, and reviews Harper Lee wrote while attending the

University of Alabama. W. U. McDonald, Jr., a professor of English at the University of Toledo and coauthor of *Language into Literature* (1965), studies this body of work and finds in it provocative foreshadowings of *To Kill a Mockingbird*.]

Perhaps unwittingly, newspaper and magazine articles about Harper Lee have given the impression that although she began writing at an early age nothing by her was published before *To Kill a Mockingbird*. Actually, however, as an undergraduate at the University of Alabama (1945–49), she wrote for the college humor magazine several satiric pieces, for the student newspaper eight editorial-page columns, and for both a few reviews. Some of these—particularly the magazine contributions—are of interest for their comments on writers and their treatment of Southern mores.

In "Some Writers of Our Times—A Very Informal Essay", she begins by poking fun at the aspiring writer who is upset because he must cut his novel about a sensitive young man, and at the one who apparently considers atheism essential for the contemporary author. Then she ironically discusses some major necessities for a modern writer: a sadistic father, an alcoholic mother who alternately loves and mistreats the child, and a soul—preferably warped. She points out that he must usually be from a small town, preferably a Southern village, which is important to his novel:

> There must be the annual race riot full of blood & gore which causes violent reactions in his sensitive (I use that word because all writers are supposed to be sensitive) soul. A whole chapter of his book must be devoted to pondering over the holy-rollers ensconced in a tent just outside of town. And he certainly must not omit his reflections upon the way justice is so casually administered by the crooked judge in the broken down courthouse. . . . He has the chance to expose to the public the immoral goings-on in an out-of-the-way village, have himself hailed as the H. W. Beecher of the day, and instigate a movement which would do away with small towns forever.

And of course, she adds, "he must know how to write". ⟨. . .⟩

It would be premature to explore the relationship between these college writings and Miss Lee's subsequent literary career. But they obviously suggest her sharp eye for human idiosyncrasies and her alertness to and disapproval of pretension and deception, even if they do not prepare one for the portraits, drawn with affection and humor, which are among the delights of *Mockingbird.* Miss Lee's fellow students had fair warning, though. An interview published in the *Crimson-White* during her tenure as *Rammer-Jammer* editor concluded with this paragraph: "Lawyer Lee will spend her future in Monroeville (her home town). As for her aspirations, she says, 'I will probably write a book someday. They all do.'"

—W. U. McDonald, Jr., "Harper Lee's College Writings," *American Notes & Queries* 6, No. 9 (May 1968): 131–32

FRED ERISMAN ON ATTICUS FINCH'S EMERSONIAN QUALITIES

[Fred Erisman (b. 1937) is Lorraine Sherley Professor of Literature at Texas Christian University and author of monographs on Frederic Remington (1975) and Tony Hillerman (1989). In this extract, Erisman studies the figure of Atticus Finch, believing him to embody the traits of self-sufficiency and freedom from the weight of the past found in the "ideal man" advocated by Ralph Waldo Emerson.]

That Atticus Finch is meant to be an atypical Southerner is plain; Miss Lee establishes this from the beginning, as she reports that Atticus and his brother are the first Finches to leave the family lands and study elsewhere. This atypical quality, however, is developed even further. Like Emerson, Atticus recognizes that his culture is retrospective, groping among the dry bones of the past . . . [and putting] the living generation into masquerade out of its faded wardrobe." He had no hostility toward his past; he is not one of the alienated souls so beloved of Southern Gothicists. He does, though, approach his past and its traditions with a tolerant skepticism. His attitude toward "old family" and "gentle breeding" has already been suggested. A similar skepticism is implied by his repeated observation that "you never really understand a person until you consider things from his point of view . . . until you climb into his skin and walk around in it" (p. 36). He understands the difficulties of Tom Robinson, although Tom Robinson is black; he understands the difficulties of a Walter Cunningham, though Cunningham is—to Aunt Alexandra—"trash"; he understands the pressures being brought to bear upon his children because of his own considered actions. In each instance he acts according to his estimate of the merits of the situation, striving to see that each receives justice. He is, in short, as Edwin Bruell has suggested, "no heroic type but any graceful, restrained, simple person like one from Attica." Unfettered by the corpse of the past, he is free to live and work as an individual.

This freedom to act he does not gain easily. Indeed, he, like Emerson's nonconformist, frequently finds himself whipped by the world's displeasure. And yet, like Emerson's ideal man, when faced by this harassment and displeasure, he has "the habit of magnanimity and religion to treat it godlike as a trifle of no concernment." In the development of this habit he is aided by a strong regard for personal principle, even as he recognizes the difficulty that it brings to his life and the lives of his children. This is established early in the novel, with the introduction of the Tom Robinson trial. When the case is brought up by Scout, following a fight at school, Atticus responds, " 'If I didn't [defend Tom Robinson] I couldn't hold up my head in town, I couldn't represent this county in the legislature, I couldn't even tell you or Jem not to do something again. . . . Scout, simply by the nature of the work, every lawyer gets at least one case in his lifetime that affects him personally. This one's mine, I guess.' " He returns to this theme later, observing that " 'This case . . . is something that goes to the essence of a man's conscience—Scout, I couldn't go to church and worship God if I didn't try to help that man.' " Scout points out that opinion among the townspeople runs counter to this, whereupon Atticus replies, " 'They're certainly entitled to think that, and they're entitled to full respect for their opinions . . . but before I can live with other folks I've got to live with myself. The one thing that doesn't abide by majority rule is a person's conscience.' " No careful ear is needed to hear the echoes of Emerson's "Nothing can bring you peace but yourself. Nothing can bring you peace but the triumph of principles." In his heeding both principle and conscience, whatever the cost to himself, Atticus is singularly Emersonian.

—Fred Erisman, "The Romantic Regionalism of Harper Lee,"
Alabama Review 26, No. 2 (April 1973): 129–31

R. A. Dave on Tragic Elements in *To Kill a Mockingbird*

[R. A. Dave is head of the department of English at Sardar Patel University in Vallabh Vidyanagar, India. In this extract, Dave finds that *To Kill a Mockingbird* is similar to a Greek tragedy in its unity of time and place and in its conflict of good and evil.]

The novelist, in an unmistakable way, has viewed one of the most fundamental human problems with the essentially Christian terms of reference, and we see emerging from the novel a definite moral pattern embodying a scale of values. As we notice the instinctive humanising of the world of things we are also impressed by the way Harper Lee can reconcile art and morality. For *To Kill a Mockingbird* is not a work of propaganda, it is a work of art, not without a tragic view of life. The novelist has been able to combine humour and pathos in an astonishing way. But comedy and tragedy are, in the final analysis, two sides of the same coin. The novel bubbling with life and overflowing with human emotions is not without a tragic pattern involving a contest between good and evil. Atticus in his failure to defend the Negro victim, eventually hunted down while scaling the wall in quest of freedom, the innocent victim, and Arthur Boo, who is endowed with tender human emotions and compassion, but is nearly buried alive in the Radley House, which is a veritable sepulchre, simple because his father loved to wallow in the vanity fair, and the suffering Finch children, they all intensify the sense of waste involved in the eternal conflict. 'The hero of a tragedy,' observes Freud in *Totem and Taboo*, 'had to suffer; this is today still the essential content of a tragedy.' By that norm, *To Kill a*

Mockingbird could be seen to hover on the frontier of a near-tragedy. The tragic mode is no longer a monopoly of the theatre. Like the epic that precedes it, the novel that succeeds it, too, can easily order itself into a comic or a tragic pattern. Particularly after the seventeenth century, tragedy seems to be steadily drifting towards the pocket theatre. *To Kill a Mockingbird* has the unity of place and action that should satisfy an Aristotle although there is no authority of the invisible here as in a Greek tragedy. With Atticus and his family at the narrative centre standing like a rock in a troubled sea of cruelty, hatred and injustice, we have an imitation of an action which is noble and of a certain magnitude. And the story, that is closed off on the melancholy note of the failure of good, also is not without its poetic justice through the nemesis that destroys the villain out to kill the Finch children. In fact, twice before the final catastrophe the story seems to be verging on its end. The first probable terminal is chapter twenty-one, when Tom is convicted and sentenced; the second is chapter twenty-six, when Tom is shot dead—not killed but set free from the coils of life, as it were—and there is nothing really left. But the novelist wants to bring the story to a rounded-off moral end. Like a symphony it starts off on a new movement after touching the lowest, almost inaudible key, and we have the crescendo of its finale. Here is exploration, or at least an honest attempt at exploration, of the whole truth which is lost in the polarities of life. But Harper Lee who lets us hear in the novel the 'still, sad music of humanity' is immensely sentimental. Her love for melodrama is inexhaustible. Hence, although her view of human life is tragic, the treatment is sentimental, even melodramatic. However, though not a tragedy, it is since *Uncle Tom's Cabin* one of the most effective expressions of the voice of protest against the injustice to the Negro in the white world. Without militant championship of 'native sons' writing in a spirit of commitment, here is a woman novelist transmuting the raw material of the Negro predicament aesthetically.

—R. A. Dave, "*To Kill a Mockingbird:* Harper Lee's Tragic Vision," *Indian Studies in American Fiction,* ed. M. K. Naik, S. K. Desai, and S. Mokashi-Punekar (Dharwar: Karnatak University/Macmillan India, 1974), pp. 321–23

WILLIAM T. GOING ON *TO KILL A MOCKINGBIRD* AS A NOVEL
OF CHILDHOOD

[William T. Going (b. 1915) is the author of *Scanty Plot
of Ground: Studies in the Victorian Sonnet* (1976) and
Essays on Alabama Literature (1975), from which the
following extract is taken. Here, Going maintains that
the true focus of *To Kill a Mockingbird* is its portrayal of
children and their struggle toward adulthood.]

The epigraph from Charles Lamb—"Lawyers, I suppose, were
once children"—indicates the two aspects of *Mockingbird,*
childhood and the law. The plot can be simply stated: Atticus
Finch, one of Maycomb's leading attorneys, is the court-
appointed defender of Tom Robinson, accused of raping
Mayella Ewell, a daughter of the town's notorious poor white-
trash family. In this struggle he is unsuccessful—at least the all-
white jury finds Tom guilty, and he is killed escaping from
prison before Atticus can gain a hearing on the appeal. But to a
certain extent the case is not altogether lost; certain precedents
have been set. Instead of a young lawyer who defends only for
the record's sake Judge Taylor appoints a distinguished lawyer
who chooses to fight obvious lies and racial hatred so that he
and his children—and ultimately Maycomb itself—can remain
honest and honorable people. No one except Atticus Finch
ever kept a jury out so long on a case involving a Negro. And
in the process of the trial Atticus's children have matured in the
right way—at least in his eyes.

The struggle of the children toward maturity, however, occu-
pies more space than Atticus's struggle to free Tom, the central
episode. Through their escapades and subsequent entangle-
ments with their father and neighbors like Miss Maudie
Atkinson, Mrs. Henry Lafayette Dubose, and particularly the
legends about Boo Radley, the town's boogie man, Jem and
Scout learn what it means to come to man's estate. In Part I, an
evocation of the happy days of summer play, the process is
begun. With their friend Dill Harris from Meridian they enact
the weird stories about Boo Radley—how he sits in his shut-
tered house all day and wanders about in the shadows of night
looking in people's windows, how he once drove the scissors

into his father's leg, how as a not-too-bright adolescent he had terrorized the county with a "gang" from Old Sarum. Might he even be dead in that solemn, silent house, the children wonder. Miss Maudie gives, as always, a forthright answer to that question: "I know he's alive, Jean Louise, because I haven't seen him carried out yet." Although Atticus forbids these "Boo Radley" games, the children go on playing—Scout being Mrs. Radley, who sweeps the porch and screams that Arthur (Boo's real name) is murdering them all with the scissors, Dill being old Mr. Radley, who walks silently down the street and coughs whenever he is spoken to, and Jem being the star actor, Boo himself as "he went under the front steps and shrieked and howled from time to time."

In the midst of these juvenile Gothic masques the children begin to learn something about the difference between gossip and truth. When Jem tears his pants and is forced to leave them behind on the wire fence during their night expedition to peek through the Radleys' shutters, he later finds them crudely mended, pressed, and hanging over the fence. When Miss Maudie's house burns during a cold night, all the neighborhood turns out to help and to watch. Scout, who is told to come no closer than the Radleys' gate, discovers that during the confusion a blanket has been thrown round her shoulders. Jem realizes that this thoughtful act was not performed by Mr. or Mrs. Radley, who have long been dead, and he saw Mr. Nathan, Boo's brother and "jailer," helping haul out Miss Maudie's mattress. It could have been only Boo.

—William T. Going, "Store and Mocking Bird: Two Pulitzer Novels about Alabama," *Essays on Alabama Literature* (Tuscaloosa: University of Alabama Press, 1975), pp. 23–25

W. J. STUCKEY ON THE FLAWS IN *TO KILL A MOCKINGBIRD*

[W. J. Stuckey (b. 1923), former professor of English at Purdue University, has written a study of Caroline

Gordon (1972) and *The Pulitzer Prize Novels: A Critical Backward Look* (1981), from which the following extract is taken. Here, Stuckey believes that Harper Lee's novel is flawed in its simplistic moral, sentimentality, and failure to fuse its two plot-elements (the childhood of Scout Finch and the trial of Tom Robinson).]

As a first novel, *To Kill a Mockingbird* is better than average. Despite its simplistic moral, some early scenes (in the school room especially) are well executed even though they are self-consciously cute. A rather long scene toward the close of the book (the meeting of Aunt Alexandra's church circle) is even more deftly rendered, suggesting that Harper Lee has more talent for writing fiction than a number of more famous Pulitzer winners. But nevertheless, *To Kill a Mockingbird* has major defects. The most obvious of these is that the two plots are never really fused or very closely related, except toward the end when they are mechanically hooked together: the trial is over and Tom Robinson dead, but the poor white father of the girl (whom Atticus had exposed in court as a liar and the attempted seductress of Tom Robinson) swears to get revenge. On a dark night, as they are on their way home from a Halloween party, Scout and Jem are waylaid and attacked by the poor white father. Were it not for the timely interference of Boo Radley, Scout and Jem would be murdered. It is then revealed that, from behind his closed shutters, Boo Radley has all along been watching over the lives of the two children who have been trying to invade his privacy. In addition to her failure to achieve an effective structure, the author fails to establish and maintain a consistent point of view. The narrator is sometimes a mature adult looking back and evaluating events in her childhood. At other times she is a naïve child who fails to understand the implications of her actions. The reason for this inconsistency is that the author has not solved the technical problems raised by her story and whenever she gets into difficulties with one point of view, she switches to the other.

This failure is clearly evident, for instance, during the scene where Scout breaks up a mob of would-be lynchers. This scene is probably the most important section in the novel and it ought to be so convincingly rendered that there will be no doubt in anyone's mind that Scout does the things the author tells us she does. But instead of rendering the actions of Scout and the mob, the author retreats to her naïve point of view. The mob is already gathered before the jail when Scout arrives on the scene. As she looks about, she sees one of her father's clients, Mr. Cunningham, a poor man whose son, Walter, Scout had befriended earlier in the story. When Scout sees Mr. Cunningham she cries, "Don't you remember me, Mr. Cunningham? I'm Jean Louise Finch." When Mr. Cunningham fails to acknowledge Scout's presence, she mentions Walter's name. Mr. Cunningham is then "moved to a faint nod." Scout remarks, "He did know me, after all." Mr. Cunningham maintains his silence and Scout says, still speaking of his son Walter, "He's in my grade . . . and he does right well. He's a good boy . . . a really nice boy. We brought him home for dinner one time. Maybe he told you about me . . . Tell him hey for me, won't you?" Scout goes on in her innocent way to remind Mr. Cunningham that she and her father have both performed charitable acts for him and Walter, and then the mature narrator breaks in and says, "quite suddenly" that Mr. Cunningham "did a peculiar thing. He squatted down and took me by both shoulders. "I'll tell him you said hey, little lady," he says. Then Mr. Cunningham waves a "big paw" at the other men and calls out, "Let's clear out . . . let's get going, boys."

The words "quite suddenly" and "did a peculiar thing" (which are from the point of view of the mature narrator looking back on this scene, and not from that of a naïve little girl as the author evidently wishes us to believe)—these are rhetorical tricks resorted to by fiction writers when they are unable to cope with the difficult problem of rendering a scene dramatically. The author wants Mr. Cunningham to have a change of heart—it is necessary for her story—but she is unable to bring it off dramatically. We are not permitted to *see* Mr. Cunningham change. The author simply reminds *us* that Scout befriended Cunningham's son so that *we* will react sentimentally and attribute *our* feelings to Mr. Cunningham. Further, the author fails to establish (in this scene as well as earlier) that Mr. Cunningham had any influence over the mob *before* Scout arrives on the scene. We do not see the mob react to Mr.

Cunningham. Such a reaction, had there been one and had it been well done, might convince us that Mr. Cunningham could lead the mob away simply by waving his big paw. As it is, we have to take Scout's supposed power over Mr. Cunningham's emotions and Mr. Cunningham's remarkable power over the mob—on the author's bare assertion.

A third defect in *To Kill a Mockingbird,* this one inherent in the author's simplistic moral, is her sentimental and unreal statement of the Negro problem. Miss Lee is so determined to have her white audience sympathize with Tom Robinson that, instead of making him resemble a human being, she builds him up into a kind of black-faced Sir Galahad, pure hearted and with a withered right arm. Though the author doubtless did not mean to suggest this, her *real* point is that a good Negro (i.e., a handsome, clean-cut, hard-working, selfless, ambitious, family man who knows his place and keeps to it) should not be convicted of a crime he did not commit. Although it is impossible to disagree with this view, nevertheless it does not seem a very significant position to take in 1961. It seems, in fact, not so very different from the stand of T. S. Stribling in 1933. Stribling defended his Negro's right to rise economically on the emotional grounds that he was *really* a white man.

—W. J. Stuckey, *The Pulitzer Prize Novels: A Critical Backward Look* (Norman: University of Oklahoma Press, 1981), pp. 193–96

❖

COLIN NICHOLSON ON THE DIFFERENCES BETWEEN THE FILM AND THE NOVEL OF *TO KILL A MOCKINGBIRD*

[Colin Nicholson, Senior Lecturer in English at the University of Edinburgh, is a widely published critic who has written *Writing and the Rise of Finance* (1994) and edited several volumes of critical essays. In this extract, Nicholson traces the differences between Harper Lee's novel and the film adaptation of it.]

Whereas in the film there is virtually only one mockingbird, that is to say only one victim, the accused Tom Robinson; in the novel several characters besides Jem Finch are at one time or another considered in that light. Much play is made, in the film's climactic court-room scene, with the fact that Tom Robinson's left arm hung dead at his side, the result of an accident with a cotton-gin which meant that it was anyway impossible for him to have raped anyone in the way his supposed victim had described it. The novelistic foreshadowing, which suggests that Jem Finch is also in some sense a mockingbird and that his experiences of racism have damaged him and, in his transition from childhood to adulthood, left him permanently scarred, is passed over in the film. Images which give the novel a kind of depth and range, are omitted, leaving Atticus's court-room remark to echo reductively in the film version: 'This case is as simple as black and white.'

Nor can this be attributed solely to the inevitable selection and compression which must take place in the translation of a novel into film, since this film demonstrates an ability to find correlatives for the novel's backward-looking narrative structure. Quite apart from the voice-over technique of Jean-Louise's adult voice, the film makes suggestive and subtle uses of childhood images in its opening sequence as the credits roll and before the film narrative proper begins. As a visual equivalent to the novel's adult narrator re-creating the world of her own childhood beginnings, we watch a child's hands shaping the letters of the film's title—a kind of writing—and we see a child's hands drawing an image of a mockingbird. While this image is being made, the camera pans across a watch, symbol of time passing, and itself an image which recurs in the film. Then, the child drawing the bird tears the paper, 'killing' the mockingbird and leaving a jagged image of white on black; the camera continues to pan across the different toys and objects left by Boo Radley for the children to collect from the tree-knot outside the Radley house. Spilled from the toy-box which normally contains all of these items, we see a penknife, which foreshadows two subsequent events in Boo Radley's life: the attack upon his father, and much more significantly, his slaying of Bob Ewell at the time of the latter's attack upon Scout and

Jem. We also see two carved figures, perhaps representing the two Finch children.

That toy-box forms a part of the film's own reference back upon itself in much the same way that the novel's narrative is a return to time past. On the evening of the day when Nathan Radley cements up the knot-hole in the tree, Jem shows Scout all of the objects which have been left for them by Boo. 'It was to be a long time before Jem and I talked about Boo again,' says the adult voice-over. Then a hand closes the toy-box which takes us back to the film's opening sequence. Such use of images suggests several possible ways in which film can find its own equivalents and correlatives for techniques of continuity, recall and foreshadowing used in narrative fiction.

Perhaps one of the most striking of these connects the small-town atmosphere of Maycomb ('a tired old town'), static and enclosed, with a particular tendency in the film's camera-work. On page 11 of the novel we read words which are remarkably close to the opening sentences of the film's screenplay: 'A day was twenty-four hours long but seemed longer. There was no hurry, for there was nowhere to go; nothing to buy and no money to buy it with'. This is taken almost word-perfect into the screenplay. The end of the novel's sentence—'nothing to see outside the boundaries of Maycomb County'—is omitted, perhaps because Hollywood sought a wider American audience for the film's narrowing of focus onto the theme of racial prejudice. But that oppressive, self-regarding community is explored in a variety of ways in the novel's leisurely space. Given the more intense demands of unity in film-time, such space is not available.

From the opening camera-shot, a shift from looking upwards to trees and outwards to the sky beyond, down onto the practically deserted streets of Maycomb, we gradually become aware that the severely restricted camera-movement throughout the film is having particular effects. When the children peer over the fence into the Radley house, the camera slides conspiratorially up behind them: as they move around the side of the house, the camera arcs upwards, to look down on them. In the courtroom scene the camera moves into close-up on Tom Robinson's face as he gives his evidence. Clever editing during the moment of Ewell's assault upon the children gives the impression of rapidity and confusion. And for the final shot, in a sense reversing the open movement down onto the streets of Maycomb, the camera tracks away from Jem's bedroom, and away from the Finch household. With the exception of these shaping movements, the camera is remarkably static during the film narrative; sometimes tracking slightly to the left or right, but more predominantly remaining fixed, unmoving. Even when Atticus drives from Maycomb proper to where Tom Robinson's wife Helen and the rest of the segregated Negro community lie, we see only the car's departure and arrival. In all these ways, any sense of movement is kept to minimal levels, and the overall atmosphere of stasis and enclosure reinforced.

> —Colin Nicholson, "Hollywood and Race: *To Kill a Mockingbird*," *Cinema and Fiction: New Modes of Adapting 1950–90*, ed. John Orr and Colin Nicholson (Edinburgh: Edinburgh University Press, 1992), pp. 153–55

CLAUDIA DURST JOHNSON ON GOTHIC ELEMENTS IN *TO KILL A MOCKINGBIRD*

[Claudia Durst Johnson (b. 1938) is a professor of English at the University of Alabama. She has written *The Productive Tension of Hawthorne's Art* (1981), *American Actress: Perspective on the Nineteenth Century* (1984), and a study of *To Kill a Mockingbird*, from which the following extract is taken. Here, Johnson studies the numerous ways in which Lee's novel embodies Gothic elements of terror and the supernatural.]

Virtually every external feature of the Gothic can be located in *To Kill a Mockingbird*, either as part of the action of the novel, or as an operative element in the children's imaginations. There are the forebodings of evil in the unseasonable snow, the mad dog in the street, and various ominous secrets. Miss Maudie says, "The things that happen to people we never really know. What happens in houses behind closed doors, what secrets—" Dill's imaginative creations are pure Gothic, as is graphically illustrated by his explanation of why he has run away from home. Scout relays the story: "Having been bound in chains and left to die in the basement . . . by his new father, who disliked him, and secretly kept alive on raw field peas by a passing farmer who heard his cries for help (the good man poked a bushel pod by pod through the ventilator), Dill worked himself free by pulling the chains from the wall. Still in wrist manacles, he wandered two miles out of Meridian where he discovered a small animal show and was immediately engaged to wash the camel." The most persistent Gothic element in the novel is the presence of witches, ghosts, vampires, and other forms of the supernatural, all of which excite the fear and terror that accompany the Gothic scene. The children, and even some of the town's adults, view Boo Radley as a ghost or vampire or witch to whom they attribute bloodlettings and blood sucking, as well as a host of minor incidents, unnatural and foul. Further mystery surrounds him as stories tell of his wanderings at night, during which he peeps into the windows of southern ladies. This monster, whose face reportedly looks like a skull, is a horror to behold: "Boo was about six-and-a-half feet tall, judging from his tracks; he dined on raw squirrels and any cats he could catch, that's why his hands were bloodstained—if you ate an animal raw, you could never wash his blood off. There was a long jagged scar that ran across his face; what teeth he had were yellow and rotten; his eyes popped, and he drooled most of the time." Not only has his awful punishment "turned him into a ghost" as Atticus says, the knowledge of his punishment has transformed him in the eyes of the town into "a malevolent phantom."

Boo's activities are very like those generally attributed to a community of witches:

> People said he went out at night when the moon was down, and peeped in windows. When people's azaleas froze in a cold snap, it was because he breathed on them. Any stealthy small crimes committed in Maycomb were his work. Once the town was terrorized by a series of morbid nocturnal events: people's chickens and household pets were found mutilated; although

the culprit was Crazy Addie, who eventually drowned himself in Barker's Eddy, people still looked at the Radley Place, unwilling to discard their initial suspicions. A Negro would not pass the Radley Place at night, he would cut across to the sidewalk opposite and whistle as he walked. The Maycomb school grounds adjoined the back of the Radley lot; from the Radley chicken yard tall pecan trees shook their fruit into the school yard, but the nuts lay untouched by the children: Radley pecans would kill you. A baseball hit into the Radley yard was a lost ball and no questions asked.

The Gothic supernatural, belief in which the children frequently attribute to black people alone, lingers at the back of the children's minds. Although they have been educated to disdain the belief in "hot-steams," those ghosts upon which the unsuspecting person can stumble on a lonely road, the children often speak of them with horror and dread.
　　　—Claudia Durst Johnson, To Kill a Mockingbird: *Threatening Boundaries* (New York: Twayne, 1994), pp. 41–42

❖

Works by Harper Lee

To Kill a Mockingbird. 1960.

Works about Harper Lee and *To Kill a Mockingbird*

Blackwell, Louise. "Harper Lee." In *Southern Writers: A Biographical Dictionary*, ed. Robert Bain, Joseph M. Flora, and Louis D. Rubin, Jr. Baton Rouge: Louisiana State University Press, 1979, pp. 266–67.

Bruell, Edwin. "Keen Scalpel on Racial Ills." *English Journal* 53 (1964–65): 658-61.

D'Alemberte, Talbot. "Remembering Atticus Finch's *Pro Bono* Legacy." *Legal Times,* 6 April 1992, p. 26.

Dunn, Timothy. "Atticus Finch *De Novo:* In Defense of a Gentleman." *New Jersey Law Journal,* 27 April 1992, p. 15.

Freedman, Monroe. "Atticus Finch, Esq., R.I.P." *Legal Times,* 24 February 1992, p. 20.

———. "Finch: The Lawyer Mythologized." *Legal Times,* 18 May 1992, p. 25.

Hicks, Granville. "Three at the Outset." *Saturday Review,* 23 July 1960, pp. 15–16.

Johnson, Claudia Durst. "The Secret Courts of Men's Hearts: Code and Law in Harper Lee's *To Kill a Mockingbird.*" *Studies in American Fiction* 19 (1991): 129–39.

———, ed. *Understanding* To Kill a Mockingbird: *A Student Casebook to Issues, Sources, and Historic Documents.* Westport, CT: Greenwood Press, 1994.

Margolick, David. "At the Bar." *New York Times,* 28 February 1992, p. B7.

May, Jill P. "Censors as Critics: *To Kill a Mockingbird* as a Case Study." In *Cross-Culturalism in Children's Literature,* ed. Susan R. Gannon and Ruth Anne Thompson. New York: Pace University, 1988, pp. 91–95.

Mitgang, Herbert. [Review of *To Kill a Mockingbird*.] *New York Times*, 13 July 1960, p. 33.

Schuster, Edgar H. "Discovering Theme and Structure in the Novel." *English Journal* 52 (1963–64): 506–12.

Shaffer, Thomas L. "The Moral Theology of Atticus Finch." *University of Pittsburgh Law Review*, 1981, pp. 197–204.

Unsigned. "Mocking Bird Call." *Newsweek*, 9 January 1961, p. 83.

Index of
Themes and Ideas